HOW TO
PICK LOCKS
FOR BEGINNERS

Mastering Lock Picking: The Complete Guide to Tools, Techniques, and Real-World Applications for Beginners and Beyond

Jordan H. Bennett

Jordan H. Bennett

Disclaimer: This book is intended for educational purposes only. The techniques, tools, and information presented are intended to help readers understand lock-picking mechanics and improve personal security knowledge. The author and publisher do not endorse or encourage any illegal activity, nor are they liable for any misuse of the information provided. Readers are advised to follow all applicable local, state, and federal laws. Practicing on locks you do not own or do not have permission to access is illegal and unethical. Please use this information responsibly.

First Edition

Printed in USA

Jordan H. Bennett

Table of Contents

Jordan H. Bennett

Jordan H. Bennett

Introduction

Imagine this: you're on a chilly evening walk, returning home after a long day. Reaching into your pocket, you feel the chill of emptiness—your keys are missing. A simple mishap, but one that could turn into hours of waiting or a costly locksmith bill. For those who understand the mechanics of lock picking, though, this situation is more of a puzzle than a problem. With a steady hand and a practiced technique, you could solve this lock's mystery and be inside within minutes.

This book is designed to equip you with the essential skills to navigate situations like this and more. *Mastering the Art of Lock Picking* isn't merely a guide to tools and techniques—it's a journey into understanding security, patience, and precision. Whether you're curious about the mechanics of a lock, interested in improving your problem-solving skills, or just want a deeper understanding of physical security, this book will serve as your guide.

Who This Book is For

This book welcomes both beginners eager to learn and experienced enthusiasts looking to refine their techniques. If you're new to lock picking, you'll find a step-by-step breakdown of tools, terms, and techniques that you can follow from scratch. For those with experience, the later chapters will introduce more complex locks, intermediate and advanced techniques, and tips on working with high-security systems.

This book will teach you to navigate locks without illustrations, guiding you through words and sensory descriptions alone. Each chapter introduces new concepts and exercises, helping you build tactile intuition and muscle memory—an often overlooked but critical aspect of mastering the art of lock picking.

How to Use This Book

To get the most from this guide, start with the basics and build a steady foundation. Each chapter progresses naturally, introducing concepts and techniques before guiding you through practical applications. In place of illustrations, sensory language will be your key. Listen to the subtle clicks, feel the tension, and follow the sensory exercises to sharpen your awareness and develop a "feel" for the craft.

Feel free to revisit chapters as you improve, and use this book as a practice companion. The appendices and online resources at the end will provide additional support, guiding you to communities, tools, and exercises that will deepen your knowledge and skills.

About the Author's Experience

With years of hands-on experience in lock picking, I understand the excitement and challenge of learning this art. This book brings together not only proven techniques but also personal insights and troubleshooting strategies that make all the difference in mastering difficult locks. Throughout this guide, I'll share the lessons I've learned, with the goal of helping you grow in confidence and skill.

Lock picking is more than just manipulating mechanisms—it's a skill that fosters patience, problem-solving, and respect for security. Welcome to your journey into this fascinating world, where every lock is a puzzle waiting to be solved.

Chapter 1

Understanding the Basics of Locks

How a Lock Works

Imagine a lock as a small, carefully constructed puzzle designed to prevent just anyone from entering. Within this metal housing lies a series of tiny, interconnected components—the pins, plug, and springs—all working in harmony to secure your possessions. When you insert the correct key, it's like presenting the secret code that unlocks this puzzle, aligning each piece precisely to release the lock.

The Key Components of a Lock

1. **Pins**: Picture the pins in a lock as tiny "guards" standing in a line. Each pin has two parts, known as the *key pin* and *driver pin*. When no key is present, these pins rest unevenly, blocking the plug and preventing rotation. The lock "guards" are essentially on duty, ensuring that no one can turn the lock without the right key.

2. **Plug**: The plug acts as the "core" of the lock and is the part that turns when the correct key aligns everything inside. Imagine the plug as the steering wheel of a car. It can only be turned when each pin is perfectly lined

up—just as a car can only drive in the correct gear. When the pins align, the plug is free to rotate, allowing you access.

3. **Springs**: Springs add tension to the lock, keeping the pins pressed against the plug, ready to snap back if the key isn't correct. Think of the springs as miniature door stoppers: they gently nudge each pin back into place, ready to block any unauthorized attempts. Without the right key, these springs keep the pins rigidly in place, blocking the plug from turning.

Bringing It All Together

When the right key enters, each cut along the key aligns the pins to the exact height needed to form a straight line across the "shear line" (the meeting point between plug and lock body). This alignment releases the plug, allowing it to turn freely, just as if you've cracked the code to a small puzzle.

In essence, each lock is a tiny fortress, with pins as guards, the plug as its main gate, and springs as ever-vigilant sentries. As readers progress, they'll see how understanding each part's role makes manipulating them much easier and prepares them to tackle more complex locks.

By weaving in analogies like "guards" and a "steering wheel," you'll help readers envision the inner workings of a lock without needing illustrations. This vivid imagery lets them conceptualize the mechanics, setting a strong foundation for learning lock picking techniques.

Lock Types and Mechanisms

Locks come in various designs, each with a unique structure and purpose. While they may look similar from the outside, each type has internal mechanisms that create distinct challenges for anyone trying to pick them. Understanding these differences helps lock pickers anticipate what they'll feel and hear as they work.

Pin Tumbler Locks

The pin tumbler lock is the most common type found in doors, padlocks, and cabinets. Its inner mechanism includes a row of spring-loaded pins that need to be aligned at the "shear line" for the lock to open.

- **Feel**: With each pin positioned at slightly different heights, you'll feel individual "clicks" as you lift each pin with your pick. The lock offers a progressive resistance; each pin moves independently, so you can sense them lock into place one at a time.

- **Sound**: Pin tumbler locks often produce a faint "click" with each pin set in place. This click serves as an audible cue, confirming you've set each pin correctly.

Wafer Locks

Wafer locks, commonly found in lockers and filing cabinets, resemble pin tumbler locks but use flat wafers rather than pins. Wafer locks require similar tools but respond differently due to their distinct internal structure.

- **Feel**: Wafers have less resistance than pins, so lifting them feels smoother, with a subtle "snap" as they line up with the shear line. Unlike pin tumblers, wafers usually move in a group, making the lock feel more flexible and loose.

- **Sound**: Instead of individual clicks, wafer locks tend to produce a gentle "clink" as wafers align together. This creates a more fluid sound, softer and less distinct than pin tumbler locks, giving the lock a slightly "looser" feel overall.

Disc-Detainer Locks

Disc-detainer locks, often used in high-security environments, have a series of rotating discs rather than pins or wafers. These locks require a turning motion to align the discs, rather than the lifting motion used in other lock types.

- **Feel**: Unlike the vertical motion used with pins and wafers, picking a disc-detainer lock involves rotating each disc horizontally. You'll feel resistance as each disc moves, requiring a delicate touch to ensure they're all aligned without moving others out of place. The resistance here is more uniform and smoother.

- **Sound**: Because of the rotating motion, the sounds in disc-detainer locks are more subtle, typically a soft "click" as each disc aligns. This lock is generally quieter and requires an attuned sense of pressure to detect the correct alignment.

Lever Locks

Lever locks are frequently used in safes and some high-security door locks. They consist of multiple levers that must be lifted to a specific height to release the lock.

- **Feel**: With lever locks, each lever adds a "weight" to the tension, so lifting feels heavier and more deliberate compared to pins. Once each lever is set, there's a noticeable drop or "sink" feeling as the lock progresses toward opening.

- **Sound**: Lever locks are usually quieter, but a practiced ear can detect the faint "thunk" of each lever as it settles into position. This lock type is about depth and weight, so pickers develop a sensitivity to these subtle shifts.

Emphasizing Feel and Sound Differences

As lock pickers develop, they'll start to distinguish these types based on tactile feedback and sound alone. By focusing on sensory cues—the click of a pin, the snap of a wafer, the glide of a disc—readers can learn to "read" each lock as they work through it. Practicing on different lock types will help readers build the tactile memory needed to recognize each mechanism, even without seeing inside.

By conveying the texture, tension, and subtle noises associated with each type, this guide enables readers to approach locks with a hands-on understanding, even if they're learning without images.

The Science of Security

At its core, lock picking isn't just about the mechanics of opening a lock; it's an exploration of the concept of security itself. Locks are more than metal barriers; they represent our need for safety, control, and privacy. For centuries, locks have provided peace of mind, protecting our possessions, spaces, and secrets from intrusion. To fully appreciate the skill of lock picking, it's essential to respect the importance that locks hold in society.

Psychological Aspects of Security

Security is a fundamental human need, right alongside shelter and companionship. When we secure our homes, workplaces, or even a simple storage box, we create a private space, a boundary that others acknowledge. This concept of a "secured space" is as much psychological as it is physical. Knowing that a lock guards our personal possessions or private information fosters a sense of control and reassurance.

Lock picking taps into this boundary-setting aspect of human psychology. Learning this skill involves understanding how these boundaries work and why they matter. When you, as a lock picker, approach a lock, you're not just manipulating mechanisms—you're touching the symbol of someone's safety and privacy. This understanding should guide how and when you use your skills, reinforcing that responsible lock picking respects the meaning behind the barriers you might overcome.

Examples of Security and Privacy in Action

1. **Home Locks**: Think of the front door lock. For most people, it's not just a barrier; it's a personal boundary that keeps the outside world at bay. Locking the door at night gives a family peace of mind, knowing they're safe inside. When you master the art of lock picking, it's important to remember this psychological element— the act of picking a lock is, in essence, crossing into someone's personal sanctuary.

2. **Lockers and Personal Belongings**: Consider a locker in a school, gym, or workplace. Inside might be a person's phone, wallet, or personal mementos. Locking these items away isn't just about preventing theft; it's about creating a personal zone where they feel free to leave their valuables without worry. Each lock

reinforces their expectation of privacy. As you learn to bypass locks, remember that this skill can affect a person's trust in the very security that reassures them.

3. **Safes and Confidentiality**: Safes protect some of our most private items—financial documents, personal identification, cherished belongings. For someone using a safe, there's a sense of absolute control, knowing these items are secure from prying eyes. Picking such a lock isn't just accessing physical contents; it's stepping into a deeply private realm where people store what they hold most dear.

Respecting the Power of Lock Picking

This book is about knowledge and skill-building, not violating boundaries. Every time you apply your lock-picking skills, you're working with an age-old symbol of safety and trust. Understanding the psychology behind security helps you approach each lock with the right perspective, respecting it as a barrier that holds meaning for its owner. This respect transforms lock picking from a technical practice into a skill guided by ethics and consideration for others.

Learning to pick a lock responsibly means remembering that a lock's purpose is to protect someone's peace of mind. Each practice session should be seen as a study in responsibility—practicing your skills not just to bypass security but to understand its importance. This approach helps ensure that, in your journey, you're not just becoming proficient but developing a profound respect for the value of security and privacy.

Chapter 2

Tools of the Trade

Essential Tools

Every lock picker's toolkit is carefully chosen, each tool having a unique function and effect on the lock. Mastering lock picking requires understanding not just what each tool does but also how it feels and responds within the lock's delicate internal landscape. Below, we'll explore the core tools, describing their roles in terms of feel, sound, and interaction with the lock.

Tension Wrench (or Torque Wrench)

The tension wrench is your guide and stabilizer in lock picking. Its role is to create a slight rotational force on the lock's plug, keeping the pins in position as you work.

- **Feel**: The tension wrench provides gentle feedback, pushing back slightly against your fingers as you apply pressure. A delicate balance is key; too much pressure, and the pins will jam, too little, and they'll reset. Think of

Jordan H. Bennett

the wrench as a doorstop: it holds the door (or plug) open just enough to allow you to manipulate the lock.

- **Effect on the Lock**: As you add pressure, you'll feel the plug "catch" just a bit, indicating the wrench's tension has engaged the lock's pins, setting the stage for pin manipulation.

- **Sound**: Though often silent, a well-applied tension wrench can create a faint creak or metallic hum, letting you know it's engaging with the lock's internal resistance.

Hook Pick

The hook pick is the precision tool of the set, used for lifting individual pins into position at the shear line.

- **Feel**: Each pin offers a unique resistance, and the hook pick allows you to feel this directly. When you lift a pin, there's a soft "give," and if you listen closely, you may sense the pin catching slightly, confirming it's correctly aligned. Imagine gently raising a piano key just until it presses down—that's the sensitivity needed here.

- **Effect on the Lock**: The hook pick slides under each pin, nudging it upward until it reaches the shear line. As each pin aligns, you'll feel a slight reduction in resistance, almost like unlocking a new layer within the lock.

- **Sound**: Often, you'll hear a faint "click" as each pin sets, an audible sign that the pin has aligned correctly. This sound becomes a reassuring cue, letting you know you're making progress with each pin.

Rake Pick

The rake pick is designed for quick, sweeping movements, ideal for unlocking simpler locks by jostling multiple pins at once.

- **Feel**: With a rake pick, the sensation is more fluid and loose. As you rake, you'll feel pins bouncing slightly under the pick's movement, giving a "bumpy" sensation rather than the precise lift of a hook pick. It's like combing through thick grass; each pass shifts the pins slightly closer to the shear line.

- **Effect on the Lock**: The rake pick disrupts the lock's pins with repeated, rapid movement, aligning them gradually. Each sweep with the rake provides a unique feedback loop, as some pins stay in position while others reset, allowing you to pick up on the lock's natural resistance.

- **Sound**: Raking is more erratic, producing soft rattles or "chatter" as pins bump and align. This rhythmic sound can be both a guide and reassurance that your tool is making contact with the pins.

Snake Rake

Similar to the rake pick, the snake rake's wave-like shape is designed to reach and manipulate multiple pins in a single motion but with a finer touch.

- **Feel**: The snake rake glides smoothly, allowing it to reach several pins simultaneously. You'll feel a gentle but consistent "gliding" effect, as if the pick is navigating grooves or ridges.

- **Effect on the Lock**: With the snake rake, pins are lifted in groups, and as you slide the tool in and out, you'll notice certain pins stay lifted while others bounce back. It's an ideal tool for locks with looser tolerances, where multiple pins can be coaxed into place together.

- **Sound**: The snake rake creates a smoother, more flowing sound compared to the standard rake. You may hear a gentle swishing sound, interspersed with occasional clicks as pins align.

Ball Pick

A ball pick is often used in wafer locks, designed to manipulate flat wafers rather than cylindrical pins.

- **Feel**: As you move the ball pick, the smooth, round shape gives a rolling sensation against each wafer. It's a lighter, almost "skating" feel compared to the precision of a hook or rake.

- **Effect on the Lock**: The ball pick exerts a light, even pressure across the wafers, allowing each to align at the shear line. This tool is ideal for locks where the pins (or wafers) need to be nudged gently without sharp movements.

- **Sound**: Ball picks tend to create a softer, more muted sound, with little more than a quiet "tick" as each wafer aligns. The tool's rounded surface means you'll feel progress more through motion than sound.

These tools serve as your "senses" inside the lock, translating the hidden mechanisms into sensations and sounds. When using a hook pick, for example, the individual clicks provide an audible affirmation of each pin set correctly. The sweeping motion of a rake pick, meanwhile, creates a rhythmic chatter, giving a feeling of moving pins collectively. Each tool offers its own unique feedback loop, enabling you to "read" the lock by touch and sound.

Approaching these tools with a sense of discovery will help you learn to interpret their feedback, using the subtle cues they provide to navigate and unlock even complex locks. The language of lock picking is largely one of feel, and by paying close attention to the tactile and auditory responses each tool provides, you can become fluent in this language.

Homemade Alternatives

While professional lock-picking tools are crafted for precision and durability, you can still explore basic lock picking using everyday items. These makeshift tools provide a cost-effective way to get started and are especially helpful for practice or experimentation when standard tools aren't available. However, using homemade tools requires finesse, patience, and a few precautions.

Creating a Tension Wrench

1. **Materials**: A paperclip, bobby pin, or thin flathead screwdriver can serve as a tension wrench. When bent into an "L" shape, these items can apply rotational force to the plug.

2. **Technique**: Insert the flat edge of your makeshift wrench into the bottom of the lock's keyway, applying slight rotational pressure. Start gently, as too much pressure with a homemade wrench can break or warp the item.

3. **Cautions**: Thin materials like paperclips can bend or snap if you're too forceful. Always keep a light touch and avoid over-bending, as this weakens the metal. If the material feels strained, stop and adjust your grip or pressure.

Jordan H. Bennett

Hook Pick Substitute

1. **Materials**: For a hook pick, a bobby pin or hairpin works well. Unbend one side of the pin, then use pliers to form a small hook at the tip. Alternatively, a safety pin can be shaped similarly.

2. **Technique**: Insert the hooked end under each pin, lifting gently until you feel it "catch" or align. Since homemade hook picks aren't as fine-tuned, your movements may need to be slightly exaggerated to engage each pin.

3. **Cautions**: Homemade hook picks are less precise and may lack the smoothness of a professional tool. Move carefully to avoid snapping the hook end or getting it stuck. These tools may not fit tightly into the keyway, so they'll need extra care for stable control.

Rake Pick Substitute

1. **Materials**: For a rake pick, an unbent paperclip or hairpin can be shaped into a zigzag pattern using pliers. This mimics the teeth of a rake pick, enabling you to jostle multiple pins at once.

2. **Technique**: Insert the rake and slide it back and forth, applying gentle upward pressure. Move the rake in a quick, sweeping motion, much like brushing dust from a surface. Since it's a rougher tool, expect slightly less control and more "feel" for pin alignment.

3. **Cautions**: Thin materials can lose shape quickly, so avoid excessive force or continuous bending. Homemade rakes tend to create more friction and may scratch or snag in the keyway. Avoid applying too much pressure as you rake, which can damage both the tool and the lock.

Ball Pick Alternative for Wafer Locks

1. **Materials**: A round-tipped bobby pin or the rounded edge of a flattened paperclip can work as a ball pick. If you slightly curve the end, it will better approximate the effect of a ball pick.

2. **Technique**: Insert the rounded end and apply gentle pressure on each wafer, moving it to the shear line. Use slow, deliberate movements since wafer locks respond well to steady, even pressure.

3. **Cautions**: Homemade ball picks can easily become too flat or bent, reducing their effectiveness. Monitor the tool's shape as you work, and try to maintain its rounded edge, as a flat tip will make it harder to manipulate wafers effectively.

General Tips for Homemade Tools

- **Mind the Materials**: Paperclips, bobby pins, and safety pins are soft metals that can bend and break. Use light pressure, and don't expect them to last as long as professional tools.

- **Fine-Tuning for Fit**: If your homemade tools feel loose or wobbly, try adjusting their shape with pliers to make them snugger within the lock. A tighter fit gives more control and reduces the chance of slipping.

- **Work Slowly**: Homemade tools lack the polish and balance of real lock-picking equipment, making it easy to overcompensate. Slow, mindful movements will improve control and accuracy.

- **Avoid Sensitive or Important Locks**: Practice on cheap padlocks or practice locks, as homemade tools can scratch or damage a lock's internals. Keep your focus on learning technique rather than risking lock damage.

Homemade lock-picking tools are a practical and cost-effective way to get started, but they require a light touch, creativity, and patience. While not as refined as professional tools, these makeshift alternatives can still provide valuable hands-on experience. By practicing with caution, you'll build your skills and be better prepared to use professional tools when the time comes.

Care and Handling

In lock picking, your tools are your greatest assets. Each pick, wrench, and homemade tool plays a crucial role in manipulating delicate lock mechanisms. Proper maintenance isn't just about prolonging the life of your tools; it directly impacts your effectiveness and precision. A well-cared-for set of tools gives you smoother feedback, better control, and reduces the risk of damaging the lock.

The Impact of Good Tool Maintenance

Think of your lock-picking tools as finely tuned instruments. Over time, even minor imperfections—small bends, dull edges, or rough surfaces—can affect how the tools interact with a lock's internal parts. A bent hook pick, for example, won't lift pins with the same accuracy, making it harder to set each one at the shear line. Meanwhile, a worn-out tension wrench might slip out of the keyway, causing pins to reset and doubling your effort.

By keeping tools in optimal condition, you ensure each tool "communicates" clearly with the lock. The subtle feedback from a well-maintained pick or tension wrench allows you to interpret every small click and resistance within the lock more accurately. This level of feedback is invaluable for developing the tactile sense needed for skilled lock picking.

Practical Tips for Tool Care

1. **Regular Cleaning**

   o **Why**: Locks are prone to dust and grime buildup, which transfers to your tools over time. Cleaning your tools regularly prevents debris from dulling their edges or causing friction in the lock.

   o **How**: Use a soft cloth to wipe down your tools after each session, especially after picking outdoor or rusty locks. For deeper cleaning, a small amount of rubbing alcohol on a cloth can remove any oils or dirt without harming the metal.

2. **Check for Bends and Warping**

   o **Why**: Tools like hook picks and tension wrenches can bend slightly over time, which reduces their precision. Even a small bend can throw off your feel and control in the lock.

   o **How**: After each session, inspect your tools for any bending or misalignment. If you notice a slight warp, carefully straighten the tool using pliers. Avoid overcorrecting, as excessive bending weakens the metal over time.

3. **Smooth Out Rough Edges**

- o **Why**: Rough or jagged edges on your picks can cause them to snag on pins or get stuck in the keyway, affecting your accuracy.

- o **How**: If you notice any burrs or rough spots, use a fine-grit sandpaper (like 600-800 grit) to gently smooth the surface. A light touch is enough; the goal is just to eliminate any imperfections without changing the shape of the pick.

4. **Avoid Over-Bending Homemade Tools**

- o **Why**: Homemade tools, often made from softer metals like paperclips or bobby pins, are more prone to bending or breaking with frequent use.

- o **How**: Bend these tools just enough to shape them initially, and try to avoid excessive force during use. If they start to bend out of shape, it's usually best to replace them rather than trying to re-bend them, as repeated adjustments weaken the metal.

5. **Store Tools Properly**

- o **Why**: Lock-picking tools are small and delicate, so they can easily get bent, scratched, or damaged if stored carelessly.

- o **How**: Use a small case or pouch to store your tools, ideally with individual slots for each one. Avoid tossing them into bags or pockets where they may collide with other items, which can dull or warp them over time.

6. **Avoid Excessive Force**

- o **Why**: Using too much force can not only damage the lock but also put unnecessary strain on your tools, leading to bending or breakage.

- o **How**: Practice using a light touch and listen to the feedback each tool gives. Applying pressure gradually and mindfully will not only improve your technique but also preserve your tools' shape and integrity.

Building Good Tool Care Habits

Developing a routine of inspecting, cleaning, and storing your tools takes only a few minutes after each session but makes a huge difference in the long run. Set aside time to check your tools regularly and address any minor issues immediately before they develop into bigger problems. This habit reinforces your connection to the craft, making you a more mindful and effective lock picker.

Properly maintained tools are reliable and responsive, and they allow you to build the tactile skills needed to pick locks with greater precision. When your tools are in top shape, they become an extension of your fingers, transmitting each movement and vibration with clarity. Caring for them is as much a part of mastering lock picking as practicing techniques, helping you progress from beginner to proficient picker with confidence.

Chapter 3

The Principles of Lock Manipulation

Feel and Feedback

At the heart of lock picking lies an often-overlooked skill: the ability to sense tiny, precise movements within a lock. Locks communicate through subtle resistance, clicks, and shifts, and a skilled lock picker learns to interpret these sensations as signals. Developing this tactile sensitivity is essential for mastering the art of lock manipulation. Below, we'll guide you through the sensations of pin movement, resistance, and feedback, helping you build a mental image of each step.

Sensing Pin Movement

When you insert a pick into the keyway, you're interacting directly with the lock's pins. As you lift each pin, it's essential to focus on how it moves, which is more delicate than it may seem.

- **Feel**: Imagine each pin as a tiny, weighted spring. As you lift it with the hook pick, the pin offers a gentle resistance, almost like pressing down on the soft bristles of a paintbrush. As you continue lifting, the pin will reach the *shear line*—the point where it needs to rest for the lock to open. Here, the pin feels slightly "lighter," almost as though it's floating.

- **Creating a Mental Picture**: Picture yourself gently lifting a small bead along a narrow path. Just as the bead reaches the top, it "settles" into place. Each pin requires a similar, careful adjustment, stopping just at the point of alignment without overshooting.

Recognizing Resistance

Resistance is a constant feedback loop as you work on each pin. Learning to read this resistance is key to understanding the lock's internal state.

- **Feel**: Some pins will feel stiffer than others, and this variability is your guide. When you lift a pin, it initially pushes back, a resistance similar to gently pulling a rubber band. As you approach the shear line, the tension lessens slightly. Too much pressure, though, and you risk jamming the pin, creating a rigid resistance that tells you to ease up.

- **Creating a Mental Picture**: Visualize a tightrope with just enough give to bend under your weight. If you press too hard, the rope pulls taut; if you ease up, it relaxes. Each pin is like a section of that rope, demanding just enough pressure to hold it in place without forcing it.

Listening for Clicks

Clicks are an audible sign that a pin has settled at the shear line. For beginners, clicks are a reliable way to confirm that you're making progress.

- **Feel and Sound**: As you lift a pin and it sets, you'll feel a tiny, satisfying "give" accompanied by a soft click. This sound is subtle but distinct, like tapping your fingernail against glass. Each click is a small victory, a sign that a pin has reached the correct position. If you're careful, you may feel the pin settle just before you hear the click, adding another layer of feedback.

- **Creating a Mental Picture**: Imagine stacking pebbles on a balance scale. Each pebble adds weight, causing the scale to shift slightly. When the pin clicks, it's like adding a pebble that makes the scale tip—an immediate signal that you've reached a milestone.

Delicate Adjustments: Developing the "Light Touch"

Lock picking requires a balance of pressure and restraint. The delicate adjustments needed are akin to learning to play a musical instrument, where each touch matters.

- **Feel**: Each adjustment is minimal, often no more than a hair's breadth. The ideal pressure feels like pressing the pages of a book together; if you press too hard, you lose the sensitivity to feel individual pages (or pins). The goal is to maintain just enough contact to sense the lock's response without overpowering it.

- **Creating a Mental Picture**: Picture yourself adjusting a tiny dial, inching it just enough to find the right setting. Every move is incremental, made with patience and awareness. A delicate adjustment means holding back just enough so that each pin "speaks" through the feedback it provides.

When you combine these sensations—pin movement, resistance, and clicks—you're engaging in a feedback-based dialogue with the lock. Learning to read this feedback involves patience, careful touch, and the willingness to sense each small movement. As you develop these skills, you'll find that each lock has its own rhythm, responding to your touch and giving cues that guide you forward.

Approaching each pin with a "light touch" allows you to detect even the most delicate of cues, training your fingers to sense each pin's individual story. With practice, these cues become second nature, helping you navigate locks more intuitively and successfully.

Tension and Torque

Applying tension is one of the most nuanced aspects of lock picking. The right amount of pressure on the tension wrench holds the pins in place just enough for manipulation without locking them. Mastering tension requires a delicate touch that can only be developed through practice and sensitivity to feedback cues. Below are exercises to help you build a natural feel for tension and a guide on recognizing the signs of over-tensioning.

Building Tension Sensitivity

Exercise 1: Light Pressure Practice

To begin developing the sensitivity needed for correct tension, start with a physical exercise focused on touch and control.

1. Hold a small, lightweight object—like a pencil or drinking straw—between your thumb and forefinger.

2. Apply just enough pressure to keep the object stable without bending or breaking it. Release and reapply

pressure gradually, building awareness of the smallest adjustments you can make with your fingers.

3. Transfer this light touch to your tension wrench when practicing on a lock, aiming to apply only as much pressure as it takes to hold the wrench steady.

Goal: This exercise trains your fingers to apply controlled, minimal pressure, building a "light touch" that is crucial for lock picking.

Exercise 2: Progressive Pressure Adjustment
Once you've practiced with light pressure, move on to a lock and use incremental adjustments to test the tension.

1. Insert the tension wrench into the lock and gradually increase the pressure until you feel the plug "catch" and hold. Note this initial feeling of engagement.

2. Try reducing the pressure slightly until you sense the plug loosening. This lets you feel the threshold where tension engages versus where it releases.

3. Repeat this exercise, gradually adjusting pressure within this range until you can consistently hold the wrench without over-tensioning.

Goal: By finding and practicing within this range, you'll develop a reliable feel for the precise amount of pressure needed to keep the plug engaged without jamming the pins.

Understanding Over-Tensioning and Its Consequences

When too much pressure is applied to the tension wrench, the pins become rigidly locked, jamming against the plug and making it difficult or impossible to lift them individually. This "over-tensioning" is one of the most common challenges for beginners and can cause frustration and mistakes.

The   Sensation   of   Over-Tensioning
Over-tensioning feels like a rigid, almost stuck sensation when you try to move the pins. Imagine pulling a zipper too fast and jamming it—the more you pull, the more resistance you feel. In a lock, this jamming effect occurs because excess tension pushes the pins tightly against the plug, making it difficult to manipulate them individually.

Exercise 3: Tension Release Practice
This exercise helps you learn to "reset" tension when you feel signs of over-tensioning.

1. Apply light pressure to the tension wrench, just enough to engage the plug.

2. Gradually increase the pressure until you start to feel resistance in the pins. At this point, if you try to lift a pin and feel excessive stiffness or tightness, it's likely due to over-tensioning.

3. Practice releasing the tension by easing up on the wrench and allowing the pins to reset. Try picking the lock again with slightly less tension, finding a balance between enough tension to keep pins in place and little enough to avoid jamming.

Goal: This exercise encourages you to recognize the sensation of over-tensioning and to quickly reset without frustration, developing a habit of light, flexible tension.

Exercise 4: Visualizing Torque in Motion
Sometimes visualizing tension can help improve your control over torque.

1. Imagine your fingers turning a fragile dial, where even a slight twist could cause it to break. As you apply tension to the lock, maintain this image, using the lightest touch to "turn the dial" just enough to engage without overdoing it.

2. Transfer this image to the lock, aiming to keep your touch as light and responsive as possible while maintaining just enough control over the tension wrench.

Goal: Visualization can be a powerful way to help maintain a light touch, encouraging your mind to be mindful of every small movement and adjustment.

These exercises train both physical sensitivity and mental awareness of tension, preparing you to balance pressure precisely. With practice, this understanding will become second nature, letting you sense when you're applying too much or too little torque, building confidence and efficiency in your lock picking.

Sensory Exercises

Mastering lock picking is largely about developing "feel"—the ability to detect the subtle feedback that each lock provides. The following exercises are designed to help you recognize and interpret these feedback cues through guided practice. Starting with basic techniques, these exercises progress to more complex routines, helping you build the muscle memory essential for becoming a skilled lock picker.

Exercise 1: Tension Control

This first exercise focuses on applying and adjusting tension, one of the most crucial elements in lock picking.

1. Insert a tension wrench into a simple practice lock or a low-security padlock.

2. Slowly increase pressure on the wrench, feeling for the initial resistance as the plug begins to engage.

3. Practice applying just enough tension so the plug holds in place without jamming the pins. Too much pressure will lock the pins in place; too little will allow them to reset.

4. Repeat until you can maintain consistent, light tension that balances control with flexibility.

Goal: This exercise builds an intuitive feel for the correct amount of tension needed. Light, steady tension is essential for interpreting pin feedback accurately.

Exercise 2: Pin-by-Pin Lifting
This exercise trains you to feel each pin's unique movement and resistance.

1. Use a hook pick to lift each pin individually. Start with the pin closest to you, gently lifting it until you feel resistance.

2. Practice feeling the "click" or slight give as each pin reaches the shear line. Focus on how much pressure it takes to move each pin and how each one "settles" when it's properly set.

3. Release the tension slightly, allowing the pins to reset, then repeat with a different pin. Continue this until you feel comfortable recognizing each pin's distinct feedback.

Goal: By practicing individual pin lifting, you'll start to detect the unique resistance and "set" of each pin, training your fingers to sense when each is in place.

Exercise 3: Listening for Clicks
Sound is a subtle but powerful cue in lock picking, often signalling that a pin has reached the correct position.

1. Using a practice lock with clear clicks (like a pin tumbler lock), lift each pin until you hear a soft "click."

Focus on the sensation of the pin setting just before the sound.

2. Practice lifting and releasing each pin multiple times to develop an ear for this click and an understanding of when a pin is properly set.

3. Try applying different amounts of tension to observe how it affects the sound and feeling of each pin's set.

Goal: This exercise helps you recognize and interpret the subtle clicks as feedback, refining your auditory awareness in lock picking.

Exercise 4: Raking for Sensitivity
Raking introduces a looser technique, allowing you to experience how multiple pins respond simultaneously.

1. Using a rake pick, insert it into the lock and gently slide it back and forth while applying light tension.

2. Pay attention to the slight vibrations or "bumps" as the rake moves over the pins. Each pin's resistance will vary, allowing you to feel some pins aligning while others reset.

3. Practice maintaining a smooth, light rhythm, adjusting the rake's pressure and speed to notice how pins respond differently.

Goal: Raking allows you to practice the concept of "feeling" multiple pins at once, helping you to gauge when some pins may be close to setting even as others are not.

Exercise 5: Progressive Lock Picking
Once you feel comfortable with individual feedback cues, try picking locks with varying pin counts or security levels to develop comprehensive muscle memory.

1. Start with a simple three-pin lock and gradually progress to locks with more pins or those with security features, like spool pins.

2. With each new lock, use your previous exercises— tension control, pin-by-pin lifting, listening for clicks, and raking—to adapt to the new feedback cues.

3. As you progress, aim to pick each lock smoothly and without interruptions, combining all feedback cues into a single, fluid process.

Goal: This final exercise integrates all the skills you've practiced, helping you build the muscle memory and sensory awareness needed for more challenging locks.

These exercises progress from individual pin awareness to whole-lock feedback, allowing readers to build tactile skills gradually and confidently. Practicing these steps will help readers develop both the sensitivity and consistency required for effective lock picking.

Jordan H. Bennett

Chapter 4

Beginner Techniques

Single Pin Picking (SPP)

Single Pin Picking (SPP) is the foundational technique in lock picking, where each pin is manipulated one at a time to reach the lock's shear line. This method requires patience, a steady hand, and a keen sense of feel. Below, we'll walk through the SPP process step-by-step, teaching you how to recognize when each pin is set correctly and how to troubleshoot common challenges along the way.

Step-by-Step Guide to Single Pin Picking

Step 1: Apply Light Tension
Begin by inserting the tension wrench into the bottom of the keyway. Apply light pressure to create just enough torque to engage the plug without over-tensioning the pins.

Tip: Think of this pressure as holding a delicate glass with just enough force not to drop it. If you're too forceful, the pins will jam, making it harder to lift them individually.

Step 2: Locate the First Pin
Insert a hook pick into the keyway and move it to the back of the lock. Slowly draw the pick forward until you locate the first

pin. Take note of the resistance each pin offers as you move the pick along.

Tip: Picture each pin as a tiny "door" that needs lifting to the correct height. Approach it gently, as if you're testing to see if it's already in place.

Step 3: Lift the First Pin

Using the hook pick, lift the first pin gently, applying slight upward pressure. You'll feel resistance as the pin rises, and then a moment of reduced tension as it reaches the shear line. If done correctly, the pin will "set" and no longer push back.

Tip: Think of this as balancing a marble on a small platform. Lift just enough to reach stability, where the pin no longer falls back down.

Step 4: Listen for Feedback

Each pin has a distinct "click" when it reaches the shear line, indicating it's correctly set. If you don't hear a click, try gently nudging the pin until it offers feedback. This click is your auditory confirmation that you're on the right track.

Tip: Not every lock produces a loud click; in some cases, the feedback may feel more like a soft "settling" of the pin.

Step 5: Move to the Next Pin

After setting the first pin, move the pick forward to locate the next pin. Apply the same gentle lift, feeling for the shear line as you go. Repeat this process pin by pin until all pins are set, allowing the plug to turn and the lock to open.

Tip: Take your time with each pin. Rushing can cause pins to reset, forcing you to start over.

Common Missteps in Single Pin Picking and How to Correct Them

1. Over-Tensioning

Problem: Applying too much tension causes the pins to jam, making them difficult to lift individually. Over-tensioning is a common issue for beginners.

Solution: Reduce the pressure on the tension wrench, aiming for a "light touch." If you find the pins are resisting too much, release the tension slightly and try again. Practice keeping consistent, minimal tension throughout the picking process.

2. Pin Slipping Back

Problem: When a pin slips back down after being set, it indicates that the tension may not be holding properly or that the pick didn't lift the pin high enough.

Solution: Revisit the tension, making sure it's steady but light. When lifting the pin, ensure it reaches the shear line completely. Listen for the click or feel for the "set" to confirm the pin is in place before moving on.

3. Oversetting Pins

Problem: Lifting a pin too high can cause it to bind, making it harder to progress with the remaining pins. Oversetting often results in a jammed lock that feels rigid.

Solution: If you sense you've overset a pin, release tension briefly to reset the pins, then begin again with a lighter touch. Focus on lifting each pin just until it reaches the shear line and "floats," avoiding excessive force.

4. Misreading Feedback

Problem: Beginners may mistake resistance for a set pin, moving on before the pin has reached the shear line.

Solution: Familiarize yourself with the subtle differences in feedback. A set pin usually offers a slight click or a feeling of stability, while an unset pin will continue pushing back. Practice feeling for these cues, even on easier locks, to build confidence in reading feedback.

Developing Confidence in Single Pin Picking

Single Pin Picking is as much about patience as it is about technique. As you practice, focus on building a light touch and interpreting the subtle cues each pin provides. Over time, you'll develop a natural feel for pin setting and learn to avoid common missteps, becoming more efficient and confident with each attempt.

By following these steps and staying mindful of common mistakes, you'll gain the foundation needed to pick even more challenging locks, mastering the art of SPP one pin at a time.

Raking Techniques

Raking is a lock-picking technique that relies on sweeping, quick motions to manipulate multiple pins simultaneously. Unlike Single Pin Picking (SPP), where each pin is lifted individually, raking involves moving a pick in and out of the lock's keyway to jostle the pins toward the shear line in a fluid, repetitive motion. This technique is especially useful for simpler locks or situations where time is a factor. Below, we'll explore how raking differs from SPP and provide descriptions to help you visualize and practice the process.

How Raking Differs in Feel and Approach

In SPP, the focus is on precision and tactile sensitivity, lifting each pin with a steady hand and listening for individual feedback cues. Raking, on the other hand, is a looser, more generalized technique. Rather than setting pins one by one, you're "rocking" and "sliding" the pick across the pins, allowing their natural resistance to guide them toward alignment.

Feel: Raking feels less structured and more rhythmic. Instead of feeling each pin's individual resistance, you'll sense an overall "bumping" or "vibration" as the pick sweeps across multiple pins. This looser grip lets you engage with the lock in a more dynamic, fluid way, sensing how groups of pins respond to the motion rather than focusing on each pin.

When to Use Raking: Raking is effective for basic padlocks, low-security locks, or situations where you need a quick entry. It's often the first technique attempted on a new lock to see if the pins will fall into place with minimal effort. Raking can also help you identify locks that require a more precise approach, as it may quickly reveal which pins are more stubborn or require Single Pin Picking.

Raking Techniques: Sliding and Rocking Movements

To help you master the feel of raking, here are two main motions to focus on: *sliding* and *rocking*.

Sliding Motion
Sliding the pick is one of the simplest raking techniques. Here, you insert the pick to the back of the keyway, then pull it out toward you in a smooth, continuous motion.

1. Insert the rake pick fully into the keyway, ensuring it touches the pins.

2. Apply light tension, just enough to feel the plug catch without jamming.

3. Slide the pick back toward you, maintaining steady pressure. As it moves over each pin, you'll feel them "bump" along the rake's teeth, aligning some while others reset.

4. Repeat this in-and-out sliding motion several times, keeping the rhythm steady but not forceful.

Visualizing the Motion: Imagine combing your fingers through sand, feeling the grit of each grain as you move. The rake moves in a similar way, gently lifting and lowering the pins as it slides.

Rocking Motion

The rocking motion adds a bit more finesse to raking. Instead of a straight slide, the pick is rocked or tilted slightly as it moves through the keyway, mimicking the natural cut of a key.

1. Insert the pick and tilt it slightly upward or downward, depending on the pin configuration.

2. Apply tension, then move the pick in a rocking motion, tilting it back and forth as you pull it out.

3. This rocking motion encourages some pins to lift higher while others reset, creating a wave-like movement that may set pins more effectively.

4. Repeat the rocking motion while adjusting the angle of the pick slightly, observing how different angles affect pin alignment.

Visualizing the Motion: Picture a seesaw or wave motion, where one side dips down as the other rises. The rocking pick lifts certain pins while others stay low, working together to bring each pin toward the shear line.

Tips for Effective Raking

- **Keep It Light:** Raking requires less tension than SPP. Heavy tension can block the pins from moving freely, so aim for a gentle, consistent pressure on the tension wrench.

- **Rhythm Matters:** Raking is about finding a steady rhythm that allows the pins to respond naturally to the pick. Experiment with the speed and pressure of your motions until you sense the pins aligning.

- **Adjust and Adapt:** If you find the lock isn't opening after a few passes, adjust the angle or depth of your rake. Sometimes a slight variation in how you hold the pick can make all the difference.

Raking is a fast, adaptable technique that introduces a unique way of feeling out a lock. By mastering the sliding and rocking motions, you'll develop the ability to assess a lock's response quickly, making raking a valuable technique for both beginners and advanced lock pickers.

Common Mistakes to Avoid

As with any skill, lock picking comes with its share of challenges, especially for beginners. Common mistakes can be frustrating but are essential learning experiences that sharpen your technique and build your patience. Below, we'll outline some of the primary mistakes to watch for, how to recognize them, and how to treat each as an opportunity to improve.

1. Over-Tensioning the Wrench

Frustration: One of the most frequent mistakes is applying too much tension to the wrench, causing the pins to jam tightly in the lock. This not only makes lifting each pin difficult but can also create the impression that the lock is "impossible" to pick.

Recognizing the Mistake: If the pins feel completely stuck and resist movement, there's a good chance you're over-tensioning. Releasing the tension slightly should allow the pins to respond again, helping you feel their movement.

Learning Moment: Treat over-tensioning as a chance to refine your "light touch." Learning to adjust tension carefully will improve your overall control and help you develop a more intuitive feel for each lock.

2. Rushing the Picking Process

Frustration: Beginners are often eager to see results, leading them to rush through the picking process or skip steps. This impatience can result in oversetting pins, using too much force, or missing subtle feedback cues.

Recognizing the Mistake: If you find that the lock isn't opening after repeated attempts, take a moment to slow down. Notice if you're moving quickly without fully feeling each pin's response, as this often indicates rushing.

Learning Moment: Use this as a reminder to approach each lock with patience. Slow, deliberate movements help you become aware of the lock's individual characteristics, a crucial step in becoming an effective picker.

3. Ignoring Feedback Cues

Frustration: Locks communicate through small clicks, resistance, and settling, which are essential to guiding your progress. Beginners may ignore or overlook these cues, focusing solely on forcing the lock open rather than listening to feedback.

Recognizing the Mistake: If you're not hearing or feeling any feedback from the pins, you may be pushing too hard or skipping over cues. Stop and try again with a lighter, more responsive approach.

Learning Moment: Feedback cues are your guide inside the lock. This mistake is an opportunity to practice sensitivity, training yourself to listen to the lock's subtle responses. Over time, you'll learn to trust these cues as reliable indicators of your progress.

4. Oversetting Pins

Frustration: Oversetting occurs when a pin is lifted too high, jamming it against the lock's housing. This often happens when too much force is applied, causing the lock to feel rigid and unresponsive.

Recognizing the Mistake: If the lock suddenly feels "stuck" and no pins will budge, it's likely you've overset one or more pins. Gently release the tension to reset the pins, then start again with a lighter touch.

Learning Moment: Oversetting teaches you the value of precision and gentleness. By practicing with smaller, controlled movements, you'll develop the discipline to lift each pin just enough without overshooting.

5. Becoming Frustrated and Giving Up

Frustration: The natural urge to "give up" can arise after repeated attempts without success. Frustration is common among beginners, especially when learning to interpret feedback and control tension.

Recognizing the Mistake: If you're feeling frustrated or ready to give up, take a moment to step back. Recognize this feeling as a sign that you may need a short break before continuing.

Learning Moment: Lock picking requires patience and persistence. Use moments of frustration as reminders to pace yourself. Practicing with regular breaks allows you to return with a fresh perspective, keeping frustration from becoming an obstacle to progress.

Turning Mistakes into Learning Opportunities

It's normal to encounter setbacks, especially when learning something as precise as lock picking. The key to growth lies in reframing mistakes as valuable learning moments. Each mistake reveals an area for improvement, whether it's lightening your touch, adjusting tension, or recognizing feedback cues. By approaching these challenges with curiosity and patience, you'll find that mistakes become stepping stones, helping you develop skill, sensitivity, and confidence over time.

With persistence, practice, and the willingness to learn from each error, you'll steadily refine your technique, becoming a more proficient and adaptable lock picker. Mistakes are part of the journey, teaching you the nuances of each lock and bringing you one step closer to mastery.

Chapter 5

Intermediate Techniques and Practice

Advanced Tools and Techniques

As you progress in lock picking, you'll encounter locks that require a more refined approach. Advanced tools are designed to tackle complex mechanisms, high-security locks, and challenging pin configurations that may resist basic techniques. Below, we'll explore some of these tools, their specific functions, the locks they're best suited for, and how they differ in feel from beginner tools.

1. The Peterson Hook

The Peterson Hook is a more refined version of the standard hook pick, often crafted with a slimmer profile and a sharper angle. This design provides increased precision and control, making it ideal for locks with narrow keyways or tightly spaced pins.

- **Best Suited For:** High-security pin tumbler locks, locks with spools or serrated pins, and locks where standard picks may be too bulky.

- **Feel in Action:** The Peterson Hook feels lighter and more agile than a basic hook, allowing for delicate movements within confined spaces. It requires a steady, controlled touch, enabling you to lift pins with greater accuracy and sense minute feedback. When using it, you may feel a sharper click or more pronounced feedback as each pin aligns.

2. The Snake Rake
The Snake Rake is an advanced raking tool with a wavy design, making it effective for locks with varying pin heights. Unlike the basic rake, the Snake Rake's shape allows it to manipulate multiple pins at once, aligning them through a rolling motion.

- **Best Suited For:** Locks with medium to low-security pins, or as a quick way to test if a lock will respond to raking.

- **Feel in Action:** The Snake Rake has a distinct "gliding" sensation, sliding over pins in a wave-like motion. You'll notice a smoother interaction with pins, especially when adjusting the rocking angle. The feedback from this tool is softer and less distinct, requiring a rhythmic, fluid hand motion to feel progress.

3. The Bogota Rake
The Bogota Rake is known for its unique "hump" shape, which allows it to work efficiently through a combination of raking and single-pin manipulation. Often used as a multi-purpose pick, it provides an adaptable approach that combines aspects of both raking and precision picking.

- **Best Suited For:** Simple to medium-security locks, especially those that respond well to a hybrid raking/setting motion.

- **Feel in Action:** The Bogota Rake feels like a hybrid between a hook and a rake. As you pull it through the keyway, it gives a mix of feedback from multiple pins, with an occasional distinct click as certain pins set. This tool allows for more dynamic movement than standard rakes, making it ideal for intermediate pickers.

4. The Diamond Pick

The Diamond Pick features a small, pointed head designed to lift pins in locks that may require more precision than a rake can offer. This tool is especially useful for wafer locks and some disc-detainer locks, where a standard hook might struggle to provide the right angle.

- **Best Suited For:** Wafer locks, locks with tight spaces, and those requiring angled lifts.

- **Feel in Action:** The Diamond Pick has a pointed, almost "chiseled" feel, making it ideal for angling pins precisely. You may notice a sharper, more direct contact with each pin, providing clear feedback on how each pin aligns with the shear line. The sensation is one of firm control, allowing for distinct pin-by-pin setting.

5. The Ball Pick

The Ball Pick has a round or double-ball end, designed for wafer locks, where lifting entire wafers rather than individual pins is necessary. Its rounded head lets it apply even pressure across multiple wafers, making it ideal for specific lock types.

- **Best Suited For:** Wafer locks and disc-detainer locks.

- **Feel in Action:** The Ball Pick feels smoother, almost "rolling" over wafers as it aligns them. Unlike pin picks, which provide sharper clicks, the feedback here is softer and more gradual, as if pressing down on cushioned resistance. This tool is gentler and requires a steady hand to detect alignment.

Advanced tools feel more precise and responsive compared to beginner picks. They're crafted with specific shapes and angles to fit varied lock designs, requiring more control and a refined touch. Each advanced tool allows for a closer "dialogue" with the lock's feedback, with distinct sensations that can help you interpret each lock's characteristics.

Using these tools effectively is about learning to sense and adapt to subtle feedback, mastering your control over each pick's unique movements. This advanced layer of tactile understanding will improve both your skill and adaptability, preparing you for high-security locks and more complex mechanisms.

With practice, these tools will become extensions of your skill, helping you approach intricate locks with confidence and precision.

Handling Complex Locks

When advancing to more secure locks, you'll encounter pins designed specifically to make picking more challenging. These security pins, such as spools and serrated pins, create unique feedback that differs significantly from standard pins. Learning to recognize and respond to these sensations is crucial for progressing in lock picking. Below, we'll explore the "feel" of security pins and use analogies to help you understand the feedback they provide.

Understanding the Feel of Security Pins

1. Spool Pins

Spool pins are shaped like tiny spools of thread, with narrow centers and wider ends. Their shape causes a distinct "false set" that can mislead pickers into thinking they've successfully set a pin, only for the lock to remain engaged.

- **Feel:** As you lift a spool pin, you'll feel an initial resistance as it begins to move. Once it reaches its narrow center, the tension wrench will suddenly drop slightly, creating a "false set." This drop feels like a small "click" or shift in the plug, but without actually setting the pin. When in this false set, you'll experience a back-and-forth wobble, as if the pin is "teetering" on the narrow part of the spool.

- **Analogy:** Imagine balancing a pencil on its eraser. As you tilt the pencil slightly, it begins to fall, giving the sensation of a quick "drop." A spool pin produces a similar effect, where the tension suddenly shifts, signaling a false set. Your goal is to gently nudge the spool pin past this "balance point" to fully set it.

2. Serrated Pins

Serrated pins are designed with multiple ridges, causing them to "catch" at various points as you lift them. This type of pin creates multiple stopping points that feel like a series of small clicks, which can make it challenging to know when the pin is actually set.

- **Feel:** As you lift a serrated pin, you'll encounter a sequence of tiny "clicks" as each ridge catches in the shear line. This makes it feel like the pin is setting, even when it hasn't reached the shear line yet. Serrated pins can feel slightly gritty or "jumpy," providing a layered resistance rather than the smooth lift of a standard pin.

- **Analogy:** Picture a zipper on a slightly rough track, where each ridge "catches" momentarily as it moves up. A serrated pin provides similar feedback, where each ridge clicks into place before reaching the actual shear line. These small catches can be deceptive, so it's important to lift carefully to feel the final set without overshooting.

3. Standard Pins vs. Security Pins

Standard pins, by contrast, offer a more straightforward lifting experience. They provide a single, smooth resistance as they move upward, and once set, they don't create a false set or extra clicks.

- **Feel of Standard Pins:** Standard pins tend to lift smoothly and click once when set. They don't exhibit the "teetering" of spool pins or the series of clicks found in serrated pins. With practice, the fluid, consistent feedback of a standard pin becomes easily distinguishable from the "staged" resistance of security pins.

- **Analogy for Comparison:** Think of lifting a standard pin as pulling a rope over a pulley—it's a single, even motion. Security pins, however, feel more like navigating a rocky path, with unexpected dips and catches that interrupt the movement.

How to Approach Security Pins

When working with security pins, patience and attention to detail are key. Since security pins are specifically designed to create deceptive feedback, practicing on locks with both standard and security pins will help you recognize these subtle differences more intuitively.

1. **Experiment with Light Tension:** Security pins respond best to light tension. Too much pressure can cause them to bind prematurely, making it harder to sense their unique feedback.

2. **Practice Recovering from False Sets:** False sets are common with spool pins. When you feel the wrench drop suddenly, pause and try "nudging" the pin gently upward to move past the false set without oversetting.

3. **Listen and Feel for Unique Feedback:** Use each lift and click as an opportunity to understand the pin's characteristics. Over time, you'll learn to distinguish the soft, singular click of a standard pin from the layered, complex feedback of security pins.

Learning to interpret the feedback of security pins builds sensitivity and control, preparing you for more complex locks with diverse pin configurations. By approaching each pin with awareness and precision, you'll develop the skills needed to navigate these challenging pins and confidently handle high-security locks.

Progressive Lock Practice

Lock picking is a journey of gradual mastery. With each lock you open, you gain more confidence, build muscle memory, and improve your ability to interpret feedback cues. Progressive practice involves challenging yourself with increasingly complex locks to develop your skill incrementally. Here, we'll discuss how to recognize your growth, suggest lock types to tackle as you advance, and outline practice methods to keep you on a steady path toward expertise.

Recognizing Progress in Skill

Progress in lock picking is measured not only by the locks you can open but also by your sensitivity to feedback, control over tension, and confidence with various techniques.

1. **Quicker Unlock Times**: If you find that you're opening familiar locks more quickly, it's a clear sign of growth. This indicates that you've developed muscle memory, allowing you to set pins with more ease and accuracy.

2. **Improved Pin Recognition**: Recognizing the unique feel of each pin—whether standard or security—is an important milestone. If you can now distinguish between spool and serrated pins by feel alone, you're advancing in skill and awareness.

3. **Reduced Frustration with Mistakes**: As you progress, you'll find yourself becoming more patient and analytical when facing a challenge. Recognizing mistakes (like oversetting pins or over-tensioning) and quickly correcting them indicates that you've built resilience and adaptability.

Setting New Challenges: Lock Types to Conquer Next

After mastering basic pin tumbler locks, advancing to more complex locks will keep your skills sharp and expand your abilities.

1. **Padlocks with Standard Pins**: Start with basic, inexpensive padlocks with three or four pins. These are a good introduction to the principles of lock picking without being overly complicated.

2. **Padlocks with Security Pins**: Once comfortable with standard pins, move on to padlocks with spool or serrated pins. These locks introduce deceptive feedback, like false sets and multiple clicks, which will challenge your sensitivity and control.

3. **Wafer Locks and Disc-Detainer Locks**: These types of locks require different picking techniques and tools, such as ball picks or disc-detainer picks. Wafer locks have flat "wafers" instead of pins, providing a new set of sensations to interpret. Disc-detainer locks require a rotating action rather than lifting, helping you further refine your dexterity.

4. **High-Security Pin Tumbler Locks**: High-security locks often contain multiple security pins and tighter

57

tolerances, making them more challenging. Brands like American Lock, Master Lock ProSeries, and Abus have models that include spool, serrated, and even mushroom pins, each adding complexity to the picking process.

Practice Methods for Incremental Improvement

Adopting a structured approach to practice will help you steadily improve your skills and track your progress over time.

1. **Daily Practice Sessions**: Set aside short, focused practice sessions each day (10–15 minutes is sufficient for beginners). Regular practice builds muscle memory and helps you improve faster than longer, infrequent sessions.

2. **One Lock, Multiple Approaches**: Practice picking the same lock using different techniques, such as Single Pin Picking (SPP) and raking. This variation helps you understand how each technique feels on the same lock, reinforcing your adaptability.

3. **Use of Practice Locks with Adjustable Pins**: Some practice locks allow you to add or remove pins or security features. Start with two or three standard pins, then incrementally add more pins and security types to simulate a progressive learning experience. These locks provide a controlled way to introduce more complexity gradually.

4. **Track Your Progress with a Journal**: Keep a lock-picking journal to track which locks you've practiced on, how long it took to open each one, and any challenges or insights you encountered. Reviewing your notes can reveal patterns in your technique and help you recognize improvements over time.

5. **Video Practice and Self-Analysis**: Record yourself picking locks to observe your hand movements and tension control. Reviewing the footage can highlight

areas for improvement, like tension adjustments or movement speed, and serves as a personal record of progress.

6. **Challenge Locks from the Community**: Once comfortable with standard and security pins, try "challenge locks" created by the lock-picking community. These are modified locks designed to test your skills, featuring unusual pin configurations or traps that require advanced techniques and problem-solving.

Each lock you conquer is a step forward, not just in technical ability but in patience, sensitivity, and adaptability. By setting new challenges and adopting incremental practice methods, you'll find that even the most complex locks become approachable with time. Stay committed to daily practice, track your achievements, and celebrate each lock you open as a marker of progress in your lock-picking journey.

Chapter 6

Troubleshooting and Problem Solving

When Things Go Wrong

Even the most experienced lock pickers face challenges, as each lock can present unique difficulties. Frustration is common, especially for beginners, but with the right troubleshooting techniques, you can approach problems systematically and overcome them. Here, we'll explore some of the most common issues that arise in lock picking and offer practical tips for identifying and solving each one.

Common Issues in Lock Picking and Troubleshooting Tips

1. Over-Tensioning

Issue: Applying too much tension is a frequent problem for beginners. Over-tensioning locks the pins tightly against the plug, making them difficult to lift and creating a sense that the lock is "stuck."

Troubleshooting: If you notice that pins won't budge or the plug feels rigid, release the tension slightly and then try again. Aim for a light, consistent touch; think of holding a pen with just enough grip to write smoothly. Practicing with very light tension can help you get a feel for this balance, allowing you to adjust as needed when pins are too tight.

2. Pins Resetting Mid-Pick

Issue: Sometimes, you may feel like you've set several pins, only for them to reset suddenly. This can be caused by inconsistent tension or accidentally oversetting other pins.

Troubleshooting: If pins reset unexpectedly, check your tension. It's likely that it's too loose, allowing pins to fall back down. Adjust the tension to be firm but gentle. If oversetting is the issue, release the tension completely to reset all pins, then start again, taking care to lift each pin carefully.

3. Oversetting Pins

Issue: Lifting a pin too high causes it to get stuck above the shear line. Oversetting pins creates a rigid feeling in the lock, making it difficult to move other pins and resulting in stalled progress.

Troubleshooting: If you feel a pin jammed above the shear line, release the tension slightly to allow it to drop back into place. Use a gentler, more gradual touch as you lift each pin, stopping the moment you feel it set. Practicing with a light touch will help you avoid oversetting in the future.

4. False Sets on Security Pins

Issue: Locks with security pins, like spools, often create a "false set," where the tension wrench appears to have caught, but the lock doesn't open. This can be misleading, especially if you're not yet familiar with how security pins feel.

Troubleshooting: When in a false set, you'll often feel a slight "give" or wobble in the tension wrench. Use a hook pick to gently nudge each pin, looking for the one that is slightly loose or feels like it has room to move. Lift this pin carefully past the false set until it clicks into the correct position. Practicing on locks with security pins will help you quickly recognize false sets over time.

5. Inconsistent Feedback or No Feedback

Issue: If you're not feeling any feedback—like clicks or shifts—while picking, it can be challenging to know if you're making progress. This often happens due to high tension or using the wrong pick type.

Troubleshooting: If the lock feels "silent" or unresponsive, try reducing tension or switching to a different pick. Start with a basic hook and practice light, controlled lifts on each pin. If feedback remains elusive, consider practicing on simpler locks until you become more familiar with how locks "talk" to you.

Identifying Problem Areas in Your Technique

Learning to diagnose issues in your technique can greatly improve your lock-picking skills. Here are some common problem areas and tips for addressing them:

- **Tension Awareness:** Many issues stem from applying too much or too little tension. Practicing with a dedicated focus on tension control (without trying to open the lock) can help. Try applying varying levels of tension on the same lock to get a sense of how it affects feedback and pin movement.

- **Pin-by-Pin Analysis:** If you often overset or reset pins, slow down and practice lifting each pin individually. Spend time feeling each pin's response and stop the moment you sense it set. This helps you identify and correct over-aggressive lifting.

- **Feedback Sensitivity:** Locks communicate through tiny shifts and clicks. If you're having trouble identifying these cues, try locks with different pin configurations or security pins to expand your experience. Practicing on a range of locks improves your ability to recognize feedback cues, even in complex locks.

- **Changing Picks and Techniques:** Sometimes, a particular lock may respond better to a different pick or approach. If SPP isn't working, try raking to assess pin positions or reset them, then switch back to SPP. Experimenting with different picks broadens your adaptability and can provide a fresh perspective.

Each problem you encounter in lock picking is a valuable learning experience. Recognize mistakes and challenges as opportunities to improve your technique and gain deeper insight into lock mechanics. By practicing patience, observing feedback, and refining your approach, you'll transform obstacles into stepping stones toward mastery.

Troubleshooting isn't just about solving a problem; it's about building resilience, intuition, and the ability to adapt to new locks and techniques. With time, every lock you pick—whether simple or complex—will add to your expertise and confidence, making each future challenge more approachable.

Resetting and Starting Over

In lock picking, sometimes the best move is to reset and start over. When a lock isn't responding or feels completely jammed, a reset can provide a clean slate, helping you refocus and approach the lock with a fresh perspective. Below, we'll discuss how to recognize when a reset is needed and share practical steps to maintain patience and composure during these moments.

Recognizing When a Lock Needs Resetting

Resetting isn't a setback—it's a strategy. Knowing when to reset can save you time and reduce frustration. Here are some signs that resetting may be the best option:

1. **Pins Feel Rigid or Jammed**: If the pins feel locked in place and won't budge with even minimal tension, it's likely that one or more pins have been overset or jammed. This is a common situation where a quick reset will clear the lock and allow you to start fresh with more control.

2. **No Feedback from the Pins**: If you're no longer feeling feedback (like clicks, slight movements, or resistance changes), it usually means the lock has lost its responsiveness. This can happen due to excessive tension or repeated errors in pin lifting. A reset will restore the lock's natural feedback.

3. **False Set with No Progress**: In locks with security pins, you may feel a false set, where the plug turns slightly but doesn't open. If you're stuck in a false set and further manipulation isn't bringing you closer to opening, resetting is a quick way to break out of this trap.

4. **Loss of Focus or Control**: Sometimes, it's not the lock—it's the picker. If you feel frustrated, distracted, or rushed, a reset can be a mental "refresh," allowing you to clear your mind and return with steady hands and renewed focus.

Practical Steps for Resetting a Lock

Resetting a lock is a simple process, but approaching it mindfully can help you avoid repeated mistakes. Here's a practical approach to resetting and starting over:

1. **Release Tension Completely**: Begin by fully releasing the tension wrench to allow all pins to reset. Let go of any applied force, allowing the lock to "reset"

internally. Take a deep breath and approach the lock again with gentle tension.

2. **Use a Light Touch on the First Pass**: As you reinsert the pick, focus on each pin with a gentle touch. This first pass after resetting is a chance to get reacquainted with the lock's feedback cues. Pay close attention to each pin's unique resistance, giving you a clearer idea of which pins need setting first.

3. **Evaluate and Adjust Your Technique**: After resetting, take a moment to think about any adjustments that may help. Were you using too much tension? Did a specific pin feel especially resistant? Make small changes to your approach, whether by lightening your touch or trying a different sequence.

4. **Visualize Success**: Visualization can be powerful for staying patient and focused. Imagine yourself successfully setting each pin and feeling the lock open. This mental rehearsal can help you maintain a calm, steady hand, even after a reset.

Staying Patient and Focused During Resets

Resets can be frustrating, especially if you're close to opening the lock. Maintaining patience is key, and here are some reminders to keep your composure:

1. **Remember That Resets Are Normal**: Every lock picker, regardless of experience, encounters moments where resetting is necessary. Treat resets as part of the process rather than as mistakes. With each reset, you're getting one step closer to mastering that particular lock.

2. **Practice Deep Breathing**: If frustration is creeping in, take a few deep breaths to center yourself. This

simple practice calms the mind and steadies your hand, helping you re-approach the lock with focus and a fresh attitude.

3. **View Each Reset as a Learning Moment**: Instead of viewing resets as setbacks, see them as opportunities to improve. Each reset offers a chance to re-evaluate your technique and build sensitivity to the lock's unique characteristics. In my experience, each reset reveals new insights that refine my approach.

4. **Limit Your Reset Attempts**: If a lock continues to resist even after a few resets, consider taking a short break or switching to another lock. Returning with fresh eyes can make a surprising difference, and practicing on another lock can reset your mindset as well.

Embracing Resets as Part of the Process

Lock picking is as much about resilience as it is about technique. Each reset is a chance to grow in patience, improve your touch, and sharpen your awareness of the lock's subtleties. By approaching resets mindfully, you'll

Patience and Persistence

Lock picking is a craft that thrives on patience and persistence, and steady practice is essential to mastery. Progress can feel slow, especially in the early stages, but every lock you attempt—even the ones you don't open—adds to your experience. I can tell you from my own journey that every misstep, every jammed pin, and every reset is a small victory, bringing you closer to understanding the nuances of each lock. It's helpful to remember that these moments of effort build muscle memory, sharpen your tactile skills, and make even the most complex locks more approachable over time.

Building patience is not just part of lock picking; it's a skill you carry into other areas of life. As you learn to quiet frustration and focus on subtle cues, you're training yourself in resilience and mindfulness. I've found that approaching each lock as a puzzle, rather than a challenge, shifts the mindset from "must open" to "let's explore." The simple act of slowing down and listening to what the lock is telling you builds patience, transforming each lock-picking session into a practice of focus and calm. This patience will not only improve your lock-picking skills but also your ability to tackle any task with a steady hand and clear mind.

Staying encouraged means celebrating small wins and embracing every lock as part of your learning journey. Some locks will open quickly; others will take multiple sessions, resets, and adjustments. It's these "difficult" locks that often teach the most. Reflect on what each attempt reveals—whether it's a new way to hold a tension wrench or a fresh understanding of spool pins. With time, the patience you develop will turn the seemingly impossible into an achievable goal, helping you face each new lock with a calm determination and growing confidence.

become a more adaptable and skilled picker, ready to tackle any lock with confidence and perseverance. Remember, each reset brings you closer to mastery.

Jordan H. Bennett

Chapter 7

Practical Applications and Real-World Scenarios

Lock Picking in Everyday Life

Lock picking isn't just a skill for hobbyists; it can be incredibly useful in everyday life. Imagine this scenario: you're at home, ready to access an old storage cabinet where you keep essential paperwork, only to find the key missing. Or perhaps you've locked yourself out of your garden shed, and a locksmith is hours away. Situations like these highlight just how practical lock picking can be—allowing you to solve small lock-related problems safely and independently. Being able to open your own locks in non-critical situations provides a sense of self-sufficiency and security, knowing that a minor lock issue won't derail your day.

Another common example is the stubborn padlock that's been exposed to the elements. Rust or lack of use can cause locks to become stiff, unresponsive, or jammed entirely. With basic lock-picking skills, you can often coax these locks open without resorting to bolt cutters or risking damage to what the lock secures. I've used my lock-picking knowledge to unjam locks on equipment storage and even open an old bicycle lock that was left unused. These situations not only save the time and cost of hiring a locksmith but also prevent the need for more forceful methods that could damage the lock or property.

Lock picking is also valuable in scenarios where quick access is essential but non-destructive entry is preferred. Knowing how to handle a stuck lock can be especially useful for caretakers, maintenance workers, or anyone responsible for managing multiple keys. Mastering this skill provides practical solutions for day-to-day inconveniences while fostering a deep appreciation for the mechanisms that protect our belongings. Through lock picking, you gain both independence and a heightened understanding of the systems that keep your spaces secure, making this a valuable skill with real-world relevance beyond the workshop.

Time vs. Technique

In lock picking, the balance between speed and accuracy is essential, and knowing when to prioritize each can make a significant difference. In non-urgent situations, patience and precision should guide your approach. Taking time to carefully feel each pin, adjusting tension, and interpreting subtle feedback are all steps that lead to mastery and a greater success rate. When there's no pressure, practicing deliberate technique over speed helps develop skill and familiarity with the lock's mechanics, setting a foundation for long-term improvement.

However, in time-sensitive scenarios—like unlocking a gate or cabinet during an emergency—speed takes on a new importance. In these cases, basic raking techniques, quick tension adjustments, or even bypass methods can provide fast access without the fine-tuning of single-pin picking. The focus here is on efficiency rather than perfection; knowing a few faster techniques can be invaluable when urgency calls. That said, speed should still be applied with control to avoid mistakes that could lead to jamming or oversetting the lock.

When facing high-stakes or urgent situations, the mindset to adopt is one of calm determination. Rather than rushing, remind yourself to focus on controlled movements while maintaining a sense of urgency. Take a deep breath, approach the lock with confidence, and apply methods you've practiced for speed, knowing you have the skills to balance quick action with deliberate technique. By training yourself to stay composed, even when under pressure, you'll find that effective lock picking is less about panicked speed and more about executing well-honed techniques with focus and efficiency.

Ethics Revisited

Lock picking is a valuable skill, but it comes with responsibilities that go beyond technique. Understanding and respecting legal and ethical boundaries is essential for anyone pursuing this craft. Practically speaking, lock picking should only be practiced on locks you own or have explicit permission to pick. This simple guideline is a foundational rule in the lock-picking community and serves to protect you from both legal consequences and misunderstandings. Practicing on your own locks, like padlocks or practice locks designed specifically for training, ensures you can develop your skills in a safe, ethical, and lawful environment.

When questions arise about the ethics of lock picking, it's helpful to keep transparency and respect at the forefront. If someone expresses concerns, be open about your motivations and the practical benefits of lock picking, such as self-sufficiency in handling minor lock issues or understanding the mechanics of security. I've found that explaining the real-world applications—like being able to unlock your own stuck shed or improve your home's security—can help people understand the practical and responsible uses of this skill. In conversations, framing lock picking as a tool for problem-solving and education rather than secrecy often clarifies intentions.

Handling ethical challenges also means knowing how to set clear personal boundaries with your skills. If someone asks you to pick a lock in a questionable situation, be prepared to politely decline, reinforcing that you practice lock picking responsibly and legally. By adhering to these standards, you not only protect yourself but also contribute to a positive image of lock picking as a skill for self-reliance, education, and ethical use. Respecting boundaries, both legally and ethically, strengthens the integrity of the lock-picking community and helps you build trust in your approach to this valuable craft.

Chapter 8

Advanced Concepts and High-Security Locks

High-Security Lock Mechanisms

High-security locks are designed with advanced features that go beyond the basic mechanisms of standard pin tumbler locks. Unlike standard locks, which may use simple pin configurations, high-security locks often incorporate features like multiple shear lines, advanced pin types (like spool, mushroom, and serrated pins), and additional security layers. Some high-security locks even utilize sidebars, rotating discs, or magnetic components, making them highly resistant to conventional picking techniques. These locks are intentionally complex to deter unauthorized access, requiring a high level of skill, patience, and an in-depth understanding of each mechanism's unique challenges.

The main difference you'll notice when picking high-security locks is the heightened feedback complexity. Security pins are carefully engineered to create misleading cues, such as false sets and staged resistance, which can make even experienced pickers question their progress. These locks may also have tighter tolerances, meaning that the slightest over-tension or oversetting of a pin can lead to a complete reset. Unlike standard locks, where each pin has a straightforward role, high-security locks often force you to analyze each feedback cue more critically, adding layers of strategy to the picking process.

Approaching high-security locks requires both patience and strategic thinking. Rather than rushing through each pin, take a systematic approach, evaluating each movement and adjusting your technique as needed. Building patience for these complex locks is a skill in itself. Give yourself time to understand the unique configuration of each high-security lock, and treat each new challenge as an opportunity to refine your focus and control. Practicing on progressively challenging locks, starting with basic security pins and moving up to more intricate designs, will strengthen your skill and patience over time. Embrace each high-security lock as a puzzle, and remember that every small improvement in technique brings you closer to mastery.

Anti-Pick Technology

High-security locks often incorporate anti-pick features designed to foil conventional picking techniques and make the process far more challenging. These features are built into the pins, springs, and overall design of the lock, creating deceptive feedback that can easily mislead even skilled pickers. Recognizing and adapting to these features requires not only technical skill but also an understanding of the unique sensations they create.

One common anti-pick feature is the **spool pin**, which has a narrow center section flanked by wider ends, resembling a spool of thread. Spool pins are engineered to create what's known as a *false set*, where the plug feels like it has partially turned, even though the lock remains engaged. When you encounter a spool pin, you'll notice a slight "drop" in the tension wrench as it reaches the narrow section, making it feel as though the lock is on the verge of opening. However, further probing reveals that the pin isn't fully set, requiring a delicate touch to guide it past this false set and correctly align it.

Another challenging feature is the **serrated pin**, designed with multiple small ridges along its length. These ridges create several stopping points as you lift the pin, producing multiple clicks that can make it hard to tell when the pin is actually set. Serrated pins tend to feel slightly "bumpy" or "gritty" as you lift them, especially under heavier tension. Recognizing serrated pins involves paying close attention to this layered feedback and learning to distinguish the final set from the intermediary clicks.

Some high-security locks go a step further with **mushroom pins**, which have a rounded shape that mimics the head of a mushroom. These pins also produce false sets, but they tend to roll or wobble slightly, adding a disorienting sensation when the pick engages them. Mushroom pins demand even greater sensitivity to feel the subtle shifts and ensure that each pin is correctly set without slipping back into the false set.

To approach these anti-pick features, begin by applying the lightest tension possible, as this reduces the risk of pins binding prematurely and allows for clearer feedback. Practice using slight nudges rather than full lifts, which helps you sense when a pin is moving into a false set or stopping mid-way on a serration. Another creative technique is to "test" the pins by gently lifting each one to gauge its response. For example, if a pin clicks multiple times, it may indicate serrations; if it wobbles or drops slightly, it might be a spool or mushroom pin.

Learning to identify these features without visuals requires patience and attentiveness to each pin's unique "personality." With practice, these anti-pick technologies will become familiar, turning once-frustrating obstacles into recognizable challenges. Developing a mental catalog of these sensations and responses will help you adapt your approach to any high-security lock, turning anti-pick technology into a valuable learning experience rather than a barrier.

Chapter 9

Building Your Lock Picking Skills Over Time

Planning and Patience

High-security locks are crafted with advanced mechanisms that can be immediately intimidating. Identifying them often comes down to a few telltale signs: unique keyways with tight tolerances, labels or brand names known for high security (like Medeco or Abloy), or visible features such as restricted or angled keyways designed to restrict conventional picking tools. Recognizing these characteristics helps you mentally prepare, as these locks will likely contain anti-pick features, unique pin types, and additional layers of complexity that require more than basic picking techniques.

Tackling high-security locks demands mental endurance and a strategic mindset. Unlike standard locks, where each pin can be lifted with relative ease, high-security locks introduce deceptive feedback, requiring you to slow down, reset often, and analyze each pin's response carefully. Approaching these locks with a "puzzle mindset" rather than a "race to open" is essential. Embrace each lock as a problem-solving exercise and take time to familiarize yourself with the unique feedback it provides. This shift in mindset not only helps you tackle the immediate challenge but also strengthens your patience and adaptability over the long term.

For a sustainable approach, incorporate high-security locks into your practice routine gradually, working from simpler security pins to progressively complex locks. Regularly practicing with a variety of locks—beginning with those containing standard pins, then advancing to ones with spools, serrations, and other anti-pick mechanisms—will steadily build your skill and confidence. Consider keeping a journal where you note each lock's quirks, your methods, and any challenges you encountered. Over time, these notes become a personalized guide to your progress and a resource for refining your techniques. Embracing this long-term approach not only makes high-security locks less daunting but also builds a foundation of skill, patience, and strategic thinking that will serve you in every lock-picking scenario you encounter.

Creating a Practice Routine

When it comes to mastering lock picking, a consistent practice routine is your best friend. Just 10–15 minutes a day, focused on specific skills, can lead to noticeable progress over time. Start with a basic padlock and work on refining the essentials: light tension, smooth pin lifting, and interpreting feedback. These "warm-up" exercises are simple but set the foundation for everything you'll encounter as you move into more complex locks. Think of it as tuning an instrument—the more precise your movements, the sharper your skills become.

Once you're comfortable, add a bit of variety to your routine. Grab a few locks with different pin counts, security pins, or even wafer locks, and rotate through them. On Monday, try a standard pin lock and focus on speed; on Tuesday, pick a lock with security pins and practice patience and precision. By challenging different aspects of your technique each day, you'll keep things interesting and push yourself in new ways without feeling overwhelmed. This rotation also helps you build muscle memory, adapt to different types of feedback, and stay sharp across a range of locks.

As you progress, throw in weekly "challenges" to break the routine and test your skills. For instance, time yourself to see how quickly you can pick a standard lock, or try a high-security lock to test your resilience and problem-solving skills. Taking on these incremental challenges keeps you engaged and offers a real sense of accomplishment as you see tangible improvements. Lock picking is a journey, and with a balanced, varied practice routine, you'll be amazed at the steady progress you can achieve over time.

Journaling and Tracking Progress

Keeping a lock-picking journal might seem simple, but it's one of the most powerful ways to accelerate your growth. A journal lets you record each session—what worked, what didn't, and those "aha" moments when you finally crack a stubborn lock. Over time, it reveals clear patterns: common mistakes you can avoid and techniques that work best with certain locks. It's like having a personal roadmap that guides you through the highs and lows of learning.

To get the most from your journal, focus on specific details. Record the type of lock (brand, pin count, security features), the tools you used, and the techniques you tried. Jot down how much tension you applied and any notable feedback—like the feel of pins setting or a false set that kept you guessing. These notes become valuable references for future attempts, giving you insights into each lock's quirks and how your skills adapt over time.

Beyond technique, capture your mindset and observations on patience, frustration, or breakthroughs. Did you try a new method? How did it feel? Tracking your mental approach can be as revealing as the technical side, reminding you of strategies that kept you focused or moments when you knew it was time to step back. In time, your journal becomes a reflection of your growth—a record of each lock conquered and every challenge met, showing just how far you've come.

Continued Learning

Lock picking is a skill that grows with you, and there's always something new to learn. One of the best ways to stay engaged over the long term is by connecting with others in the lock-picking community. Online forums like the *lockpicking subreddit* or dedicated websites like *LockLab* and *BosnianBill's LockLab* offer a wealth of knowledge, from tutorials to troubleshooting advice. Joining these communities lets you learn from experienced pickers, share your own progress, and even take part in lock-picking challenges. It's a welcoming environment that keeps learning fun and collaborative.

As you explore more advanced techniques, experimenting with new lock types can help push your skills further. Consider investing in a selection of practice locks with varied features— locks with different pin configurations, security pins, and even sidebars. Many lock-picking suppliers offer practice locks designed to be picked multiple times without causing damage, making them ideal for testing new skills. If you're interested in high-security locks, practice on locks you own or those that are specifically meant for training. This approach allows you to push your abilities while maintaining control over your practice environment.

Finally, remember that ethical boundaries are essential in this craft. Practicing on locks that you own or those designated for training ensures you're respecting privacy and legality. Avoid attempting to pick locks that you don't have permission to access, as this not only crosses ethical lines but can lead to legal issues. By staying within these guidelines, you'll foster a reputation of integrity within the community and enjoy lock picking as a skill that empowers and educates, rather than disrupts. In this way, lock picking remains a rewarding journey that continuously challenges and enriches your knowledge.

Chapter 10

Lock Maintenance and Repair

Preventive Maintenance for Locks

Regular maintenance is a simple but effective way to keep locks functioning smoothly and prevent common issues. Locks face daily wear and exposure to dust, moisture, and grime, all of which can lead to sticking pins, rust, or sluggish keyways. By implementing a few straightforward maintenance habits, you can extend the life of your locks and maintain their performance.

One of the easiest preventive practices is regular cleaning. Use a small brush or compressed air to clear dust and debris from the keyway. This step is especially important for outdoor locks or those in dusty environments, as dirt can accumulate over time and restrict pin movement. Occasionally check for signs of rust or corrosion, which are common with outdoor locks. If you notice early rusting, a gentle scrub with a wire brush can help remove it, preventing it from spreading.

Lubrication is another key aspect of lock maintenance. A dry graphite lubricant, applied once every few months, works well for most locks. Avoid oil-based lubricants, as these can attract dust and cause buildup over time. To apply graphite, insert a small amount into the keyway, then insert and turn the key a few times to distribute it evenly. This keeps the pins moving smoothly, ensuring they align correctly without sticking or grinding.

Occasional inspection is also useful, especially for locks that see heavy use. By checking for early signs of wear, rust, or stiffness, you can address potential issues before they worsen. Regular cleaning, periodic lubrication, and a watchful eye can make a significant difference, allowing your locks to function smoothly and reliably for years.

Diagnosing and Fixing Common Lock Issues

Even with regular upkeep, locks can develop issues over time due to wear, environmental factors, or mechanical fatigue. Recognizing these common problems early allows you to address them promptly, maintaining the security and functionality of your locks without the need for professional assistance.

One prevalent issue is a key becoming difficult to insert or turn. This often indicates dirt buildup or internal components starting to wear out. If you notice resistance when inserting the key, or if the key doesn't turn smoothly, it's a sign that the lock may have sticking pins or a sluggish keyway. To resolve this, start by cleaning the lock with compressed air to remove any debris from the keyway. After cleaning, apply a dry graphite lubricant to the key and insert it into the lock several times to distribute the lubricant evenly. This helps the internal pins move freely and restores smooth operation.

Another common problem is a lock that feels loose or wobbly. This can result from loose mounting screws or worn internal parts. Begin by checking the external screws on the lock and tightening them if necessary. If the lock mechanism itself feels unstable, it might indicate internal wear. In such cases, consider removing the lock (if you're comfortable doing so) to inspect for worn or broken components. Replacing worn parts or the entire lock cylinder can often resolve the issue.

Rust and corrosion are also frequent culprits, especially for outdoor locks exposed to the elements. Visible rust, a rough key action, or a key that gets stuck can all signal corrosion. To address this, gently apply a rust remover to the affected areas, taking care not to allow excess liquid into the lock mechanism. After treating the rust, lubricate the lock with a dry lubricant to prevent future corrosion and ensure smooth operation.

To efficiently diagnose lock problems without dismantling them, you can develop a quick checklist:

1. **Visual Inspection**: Look for obvious signs of damage, rust, or wear on the lock's exterior and keyway.

2. **Key Assessment**: Insert the key slowly, noting any resistance, grittiness, or unusual tightness.

3. **Operation Test**: Turn the key gently to see if the lock engages smoothly. Listen for any grinding noises or feel for unusual stiffness.

4. **Physical Stability**: Wiggle the lock slightly to check for looseness or instability in the mounting.

5. **Environmental Factors**: Consider recent weather conditions or exposure to elements that might affect the lock's performance.

By regularly running through this checklist, you can catch and address minor lock issues before they escalate. Early detection and simple maintenance steps like cleaning, lubricating, and tightening components can significantly extend the life of your locks and keep them functioning reliably. Remember, if a lock continues to malfunction after basic troubleshooting, it may be time to consult a professional locksmith to ensure your security is not compromised.

Upgrading Security for High-Risk Locks

For those looking to bolster security at home or work, upgrading your locks doesn't always mean replacing them entirely. Small, strategic upgrades can make a significant difference in protecting against unauthorized entry and make your locks more resilient to picking or bypassing methods.

One of the simplest ways to enhance security is by installing **security pins** in existing locks. Security pins, such as spool or mushroom pins, create false sets that are more challenging for pickers to manipulate. Many standard pin tumbler locks can be upgraded with these pins by a locksmith, making them tougher to pick. Adding even a few security pins can add a valuable layer of difficulty, deterring casual or opportunistic lock pickers.

When selecting high-security locks, look for models that are **rated for resistance to picking, drilling, and bumping**—three common methods of forced entry. High-security brands like Medeco, Abloy, and Mul-T-Lock offer locks with specialized mechanisms like rotating pins, sidebars, or magnetic elements that increase the complexity for potential intruders. Make sure the lock fits your specific needs; for example, residential settings may benefit from high-security deadbolts, while workplaces might consider restricted keyway locks that limit key duplication to authorized personnel only.

Finally, **additional security measures around the lock** can further fortify your entry points. Installing protective strike plates or reinforcing the door frame strengthens your defenses against brute-force attacks, such as kicking or drilling. For padlocks, choose ones with a shrouded shackle to minimize exposure to cutting tools. These simple additions can make a lock more resistant to picking and bypass methods by physically limiting access or increasing the effort required to break it open.

By combining these upgrades, you can significantly increase the security of your locks without needing to replace them entirely. Upgraded locks serve as a stronger deterrent and make forced entry methods more challenging, giving you and your property greater protection and peace of mind.

Chapter 11

Beyond Lock Picking: Exploring Other Entry Techniques

Bumping and Bypass Techniques

Lock bumping and bypass techniques offer alternative ways to open locks without traditional picking, but they require understanding, caution, and ethical considerations. These methods can be useful tools, especially in situations where access is needed quickly or picking isn't effective, but they should only be used responsibly and with explicit permission.

Lock Bumping works by using a specially cut "bump key" that fits into a lock's keyway. When the bump key is inserted and struck with a light tap, the force temporarily aligns the pins at the shear line, allowing the plug to turn. However, this technique works best on traditional pin tumbler locks with simpler security features. Locks that lack security pins, such as spool or mushroom pins, are generally more susceptible to bumping, as they don't create as much resistance to the sudden impact. To protect against bumping, high-security locks often feature more complex pin mechanisms, restricted keyways, or integrated sidebars that prevent unauthorized access through this method.

However, experimenting with bumping or bypass methods brings specific ethical and safety considerations. Using these techniques on locks that you don't own or lack permission to access is illegal and unethical, as it can compromise others' security. Always remember that these techniques are meant to be used responsibly, for educational or permitted practice only. If you're experimenting with bumping, make sure to wear ear and eye protection, as the technique involves striking metal on metal, which can produce loud sounds and potential metal shards. Practicing on training locks or locks you own helps ensure that you're using these methods appropriately.

For lower-security locks, **simple bypass techniques** can sometimes provide quick access without picking. One common method is **shimming**, where a thin, flexible piece of metal is slid between the shackle and the body of a padlock, disengaging the locking mechanism directly. This works best on older or budget padlocks without anti-shim features. Another technique is **latch slipping**, often called "loiding," where a plastic card or similar object is slid between the door latch and frame, pushing back the latch. This technique is effective for spring-loaded latches on interior doors but will not work on deadbolts or doors with latch guards.

These bypass techniques are practical for low-stakes scenarios, such as retrieving items from a forgotten locker or accessing a garden shed. However, always ensure you have permission, as ethical lock picking and bypassing are about respecting boundaries and practicing responsibility. Used responsibly, understanding these methods enhances your overall knowledge of security, helping you better appreciate the complexities of lock mechanisms and access control.

Using Specialty Tools and Their Ethical Use

Beyond basic lock picks, there's a variety of specialty tools available that offer advanced ways to manipulate locks, often in unique or non-traditional ways. These tools include items like jigglers, bypass drivers, and tubular picks, each designed to work with specific lock mechanisms or entry challenges. While these tools expand your capabilities as a lock picker, they also require a strong sense of responsibility and an understanding of ethical boundaries.

Jigglers are a set of flat keys with various cut patterns designed to mimic the effect of a key in the lock. When inserted, the jiggler is moved in a wiggling or twisting motion to align the lock's pins or wafers. This tool is particularly effective on wafer locks, commonly found in file cabinets, some vehicle locks, and inexpensive padlocks. Jigglers work by quickly testing various alignments, offering a faster method than traditional pin-by-pin picking. However, because they bypass much of the tactile feedback of picking, they're best reserved for situations where quick access is needed.

Bypass drivers allow you to engage certain locks directly, bypassing the pin mechanism altogether. For example, bypass drivers can be used to rotate the cam mechanism in some low- to mid-security padlocks, making it possible to open the lock without interacting with the pins. This tool is often effective on padlocks with exposed or accessible cam mechanisms. However, it's only useful on locks that have a known bypass vulnerability, and its use should be limited to locks you own or have explicit permission to access.

Tubular picks are designed specifically for tubular or radial locks, often found on vending machines, bike locks, and some cash boxes. Unlike pin tumbler locks, tubular locks use a circular arrangement of pins that require precise alignment around the cylinder. Tubular picks allow you to engage all pins simultaneously, reducing the time needed to manipulate each pin individually. These picks require practice to master, as the pins can be sensitive and easily overset.

Experimenting with specialty tools demands a high level of ethical responsibility. These tools, especially bypass drivers and jigglers, are often effective on lower-security locks, which may not be equipped with complex anti-pick features. Always obtain clear permission before using these tools on any lock you don't own, as bypass methods can compromise the lock's integrity and security. Practicing on training locks or locks specifically purchased for experimentation is the safest way to develop skill without infringing on others' privacy.

Certain scenarios call for specialty tools, but using them thoughtfully is key. For instance, jigglers might be used to open a personal filing cabinet if you've misplaced the key, while bypass drivers are helpful on your own padlocks that may have jammed or lost keys. When deciding whether to use these tools, assess whether traditional picking would work first, as bypass methods are often quicker but more invasive. The goal in responsible lock picking is always to respect security and use specialty tools as a means of learning or last-resort solutions, rather than shortcuts. With an ethical mindset, specialty tools can be valuable assets, expanding your understanding of lock mechanisms and enhancing your skill set responsibly.

Understanding Non-Pin-Based Locks

Non-pin-based locks, such as magnetic, digital, and combination locks, present a fascinating range of alternative mechanisms that operate very differently from traditional pin tumbler locks. These locks use unique principles, such as magnetic force, electronic circuits, or mechanical combinations, to restrict access. Learning about these locks not only diversifies your lock-picking knowledge but also equips you with skills to understand and troubleshoot a broader range of security devices.

Magnetic Locks use magnets instead of traditional pins to secure the locking mechanism. In these locks, magnetic fields are carefully aligned to either hold a lock in place or release it when the correct magnetic "key" is applied. A magnetized key, card, or fob aligns with the internal magnetic fields, activating or deactivating the lock. Because magnetic locks lack physical pins or tumblers, there's little in terms of tactile feedback. The approach here is often about understanding magnetic configurations and experimenting with magnetic keys or magnetic field readers.

Digital Locks function through electronic systems, often using keypads, proximity sensors, or biometrics to grant access. These locks require programming and circuitry, making them quite distinct from mechanical locks. Each input on a keypad or a swipe from a keycard sends an electronic signal, unlocking the mechanism only when the correct code or ID is presented. Opening digital locks often involves understanding electronic components, power supply issues, or software-based methods rather than traditional lock-picking techniques.

Combination Locks use a series of rotating dials that must align precisely with an internal mechanism to release the shackle. Inside the lock, each dial controls a small cam that must line up correctly to allow the shackle to disengage. This type of lock requires a different skill set, involving "feeling" for subtle clicks or changes in resistance that indicate alignment of the correct combination. While these locks lack pins, they still offer a form of tactile feedback and are often opened by carefully adjusting each dial while sensing for changes in tension.

Opening non-pin-based locks requires a creative approach and additional skills. **Magnetic locks** call for experimentation with magnetic tools or keys and an understanding of magnetic field interactions. **Digital locks** demand a basic knowledge of electronics, power sources, and sometimes programming skills to troubleshoot access issues. For **combination locks**, practice in "dial manipulation" is essential; this involves turning each dial incrementally and sensing the slight changes in resistance or clicks that indicate correct alignment.

For those interested in expanding into non-pin-based locks, consider practicing with **magnetic keys, electronic troubleshooting tools (like multimeters for digital locks), and combination dial manipulators**. Gaining hands-on experience with each type will help you develop a broader, more adaptable skill set. Exploring these alternative mechanisms not only enhances your lock-picking knowledge but also allows you to understand a wide variety of security systems, making you a more versatile and knowledgeable practitioner in the world of locks and security.

Conclusion

Congratulations on reaching the end of *How to pick locks for beginners*! By now, you've not only explored the fundamental tools and techniques but also delved into advanced concepts and the practical, ethical applications of this skill. Whether you're a curious beginner or an experienced enthusiast, you've taken a significant step toward understanding the mechanics of locks and the art of opening them.

Remember, lock picking is more than just a technical skill—it's a practice in patience, problem-solving, and precision. Each lock you encounter will teach you something new, challenging you to think critically and adapt your techniques. As you continue your journey, don't forget the importance of responsibility and ethical boundaries. Practicing safely and respecting others' security is what transforms this craft into a valuable, respected pursuit.

If you've found this book helpful, your feedback would mean the world to me. Reviews not only help other readers discover the value of this guide but also allow me to refine future editions and continue sharing practical knowledge with enthusiasts like you. If you feel inspired, please consider leaving a review on Amazon—it's quick, easy, and makes a big difference.

Thank you for choosing *How to pick locks for beginners!*. Here's to unlocking more knowledge, mastering new skills, and always approaching challenges with curiosity and determination.

Happy picking!

Jordan H. Bennett

91

Jordan H. Bennett

Jordan H. Bennett

Jordan H. Bennett

Made in the USA
Middletown, DE
28 December 2024

68367623R00055